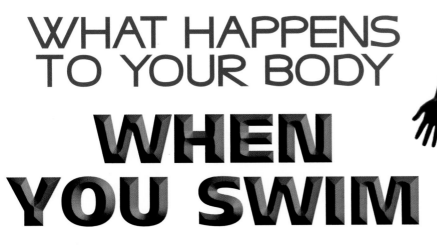

WHAT HAPPENS TO YOUR BODY

WHEN YOU SWIM

I JEANNE NAGLE I

rosen publishing's
rosen central

New York

For Scott, who swims like a fish

Published in 2010 by The Rosen Publishing Group, Inc.
29 East 21st Street, New York, NY 10010

Library of Congress Cataloging-in-Publication Data

Nagle, Jeanne.
What happens to your body when you swim / Jeanne Nagle.—1st ed.
    p. cm.—(The how and why of exercise)
Includes bibliographical references and index.
ISBN-13: 978-1-4358-5309-6 (library binding)
1. Swimming—Juvenile literature. 2. Physical fitness—Juvenile literature.
3. Exercise—Juvenile literature. I. Title.
GV837.6.N35 2009
797.2'1—dc22

                                                                    2009001043

Manufactured in Malaysia

CONTENTS

INTRODUCTION

There are people who believe that "exercise" is a dirty word. Whenever they hear the word, it makes them think about something that is hard, painful, annoying, or inconvenient. Yet all that exercise really means is making an effort to participate in activities that keep a body healthy and fit. Technically, riding your bike for fun or mowing the lawn—even walking around the mall with your friends—is considered exercise.

Improving your health and increasing fitness do require more of a dedicated effort, though. That's where aerobic exercise and strength training come in. Aerobics involve periods of constant motion that raise a person's heart rate. The activity level should be fairly intense to the point where you can still have a conversation with someone but it's a little difficult. About thirty minutes of aerobic activity, done three to five times a week, can raise your heart rate enough to keep you physically fit.

Strength training works the body's muscles using resistance, which means making them push or pull against weight or a steady, solid object. Weight lifting and push-ups are common strength training exercises. Done in short bursts of activity called repetitions ("reps" for short), strength

Whether you're racing someone or are on your own, swimming provides a complete (and fun) workout.

training tones muscles and increases your flexibility and endurance, or the length of time you can remain active without getting tired.

Swimming has been called the perfect exercise, mainly because of its inclusive, or wide-ranging, nature. Every part of the human body gets in on the act of swimming and receives benefits. An extra advantage to swimming is that it is fun. It's easy to think of splashing around in a pool or jumping into a lake as enjoyable, rather than exercise or a chore.

Not only that, but water-based workouts like swimming are low impact, meaning they don't put a lot of stress on the body. Floating in water creates a kind of cushion that allows the body to move but not feel the force of contact. Therefore, the chance of injury during swimming is much less than with other land-based exercises, where the bones and joints tend to take a pounding during activity.

As long as people are reasonably healthy to start with, know the basics of how to swim, and don't overdo it by exercising too long or beyond their ability, they can get quite fit by swimming.

What Happens When You Swim

The effects of swimming on the human body are apparent from the moment a person enters the water. The heart, for example, has a rather peculiar reaction to swimming. Being immersed in water makes a person's heart beat slower. Compared to being on dry land, people log around ten fewer resting heartbeats a minute simply by being in the water, and up to thirty beats a minute less when they are actively exercising. Scientists are not completely sure why the heart slows during swimming. One possible explanation is that because buoyancy and the body's horizontal position during swimming reduce the effect of gravity, blood doesn't have to fight as hard to flow to and from the heart. The reduced effort means fewer heartbeats are necessary to circulate the blood.

Even though a swimmer's heart pumps slower than, say, a runner's, essentially the same amount of blood circulates throughout the body with each form of exercise. Like other aerobic exercise, swimming increases the demand for oxygen-rich blood throughout the body. A person's heart rate increases when he or she swims, just as it would during running.

The heart is a muscle, and just as with any other muscle, it gets stronger the more it is exercised. After a few weeks, swimmers who are dedicated to their sport wind up having hearts that are slightly larger than normal, which makes pumping blood easier even while resting on dry land. Also, the body's blood vessels become more flexible and actually increase in number.

CHAPTER 1

Blood travels a long way throughout the body. Changes to the heart and circulatory system during swimming make the trip easier.

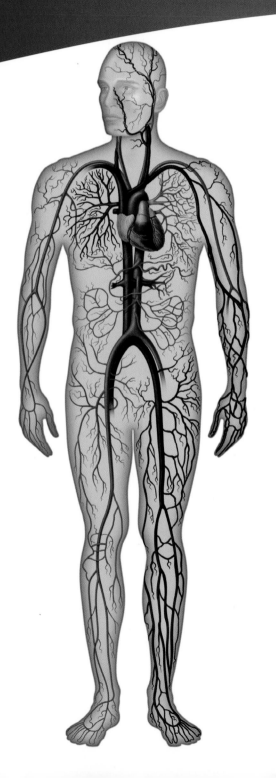

Heavy Breathing

All forms of exercise require the lungs to take in more air because oxygen is like fuel that gives the human body energy. Oxygen helps keep cells, organs, and muscles running smoothly. When activity increases, so does the body's need for oxygen to make up for all the energy being used up. Swimming increases the respiratory rate, which is the number of breaths taken per minute. In other words, breathing grows quicker when a person swims in an attempt by the lungs to gather more oxygen and deliver it to cells.

Working out in water adds an interesting wrinkle when it comes to increased respiration, which is how the body uses oxygen to create energy. Obviously inhaling, or breathing in, is impossible underwater. Therefore, swimmers are limited to inhaling only during those moments when their faces are out of the water. They have to time their breaths to get the maximum amount of oxygen possible to meet increased demand. Getting into a breathing rhythm, known as regulated or controlled breathing, is a very important part of swimming.

Revved-Up Metabolism

Metabolism is a series of chemical reactions in the body that, among other life-giving processes, converts food to energy. Exercise boosts metabolism, meaning food is converted and used up more quickly than when a person is inactive. Swimmers have very high metabolism rates. Olympic swimming champion Michael Phelps eats around ten thousand calories a day while in training. Keep in mind, though, that he's a professional. Amateur swimmers don't need to eat that much to raise energy levels.

Without it, a person will not be able to exercise for very long, and he or she will not get all the benefits that swimming has to offer.

Lengthen and Strengthen

Every major muscle group in the human body needs to cooperate in order for a person to swim. Muscles in the shoulders, arms, chest, abdomen, hips, buttocks, and legs go through coordinated stretching and contraction with each stroke and kick.

They grow stronger because they are pushing against the water, which resists, or fights, their movements. Think about simply walking through waist- or chest-deep water. Activity is slower than when walking on land because water, which is more dense than air, resists movement.

Resistance training through swimming tones, or firms up, muscles but does not make them bulky, like weightlifting can. Picture a muscle as a stretchy rubber band. When the band is contracted, or shortened, it is normally rather thick. If the rubber band is stretched, however, its sides become long and thinner. Muscles work in much the same way. Weightlifting strengthens muscles while they are contracting. For instance, doing arm curls with the elbow bent shortens the bicep muscle in the upper arm.

Swimming underwater offers extra resistance, which firms and tones muscles.

This causes the muscles to thicken. On the other hand, the stretching and reaching motions of swimming, particularly in the arms, elongate (or lengthen) muscles as they strengthen them.

Wrinkles, Water, and Oil

The reaction of skin and hair to water exercise is visible to the naked eye. The outer-most layer of skin, known as the epidermis, contains a layer of protein called keratin.

Moisture from lotion keeps hands smooth. Excess moisture from soaking in water while swimming puffs up skin layers and wrinkles fingers and toes.

When a swimmer is in the pool long enough, the keratin absorbs so much water that the skin swells. Very thick layers of keratin are on the feet and hands. These areas puff up with pockets of water, which is why fingers and toes look wrinkled while swimming.

Another noticeable change happens because the skin actually loses moisture as a result of swimming. A thin layer of oil covering the epidermis keeps tissue and cells hydrated, or full of moisture. Normally, the oil stays put—at least until some substance comes along to wash it away. Chemicals in pools eat away at the oil, but plain water does damage as well. Soaking in water destroys the protective layer of oil, allowing the skin to get dry. When skin gets dry, it feels itchy. The visible change is that people can see flaky, scaly patches or a rash where the skin itches.

Water and chemicals also strip hair of its natural oils. Unless they cover their heads with a cap, swimmers frequently find themselves with dry, damaged hair.

Peak Performance

If you would like to be a swimmer but are starting from scratch, the first thing you should do is look into swimming lessons. The ability to stay afloat and move fairly quickly through the water are basic requirements for beginning an exercise routine built around swimming.

Simply paddling around in a pool is decent exercise, merely because it involves being active. However, there are a lot more options open to anyone who is serious about getting a workout in the water. People who already know how to swim can kick their abilities up a notch by preparing, monitoring their swim time, improving their technique, and using gear designed to enhance swimming performance.

Preparation

Putting together a personalized swimming routine is an excellent preparation method. Professional swimmers and those who swim on teams have a coach to map out their practices and schedules. Amateurs, who swim for fitness and fun, generally have to be their own coaches. Although individual swimmers can certainly talk to a professional coach and get his or her advice, most amateurs come up with their own routines.

A swimming session should have three parts: a warm-up, aerobic exercise, and a cool-down period. Because it happens before actual swimming, the warm-up is

Swim preparation can be done in the water or on land. Stretching and core (abdominal) workouts are excellent preparation.

considered preparation. As with any type of exercise, warming up before swimming is key. Jumping right into the water and swimming could result in an injury, such as pulled or cramping muscles, or fatigue, which means being extremely tired.

Stretching is a good warm-up. In fact, stretching literally warms the muscles by raising their temperature, making them contract with more force and relax quicker. Stretching can be done on land or in shallow water. A lot is going to be asked of the body's muscles. It is extremely helpful if they are as loose and primed as possible before getting active. Special attention should be paid to the arms, which carry the bulk of the workload.

Weight Training

Amateur swimmers may choose to add weight training to their swimming program. Strengthening muscles increases a swimmer's speed and endurance in the water. Free weights or stationary weight machines can be used to either target muscle groups used in swimming or imitate swimming strokes. Arm and leg curls, lat pull-downs, calf raises, and bench presses work well for swimmers. If you are unfamiliar with these exercises, ask a fitness trainer how to perform them.

Technique

The aerobic portion of a swim routine is the actual swimming itself. The motion that propels a swimmer's body, or moves it forward, through the water is called a stroke. When swimming for physical fitness, there are five basic strokes.

Also called the crawl, the freestyle starts with swimmers floating on their stomachs. They reach their arms out, one at a time, in front of them with the hands cupped. The arms push down and back until they are parallel to the swimmers'

Freestyle is called the crawl because its motions are similar to those needed for crawling on land. Freestyle is swimming's most popular stroke.

sides while underwater. At the same time, the legs take turns kicking straight out under the water, performing a flutter kick. Freestyle swimmers inhale with their heads to one side and faces out of the water, and exhale through their mouths into the water.

The backstroke is similar to freestyle except that, as the name implies, the swimmer is on his or her back. A swimmer's arms reach back out over his or her head. When the backs of the hands enter the water, they are flat like the oars of a rowboat, not cupped. The flutter kick is also used during the backstroke. Because swimmers are floating on their backs and their faces never go into the water, breathing is simply timed to match a certain number of strokes.

A reverse version of freestyle, the backstroke incorporates a slightly different way to breathe than other strokes.

For the breaststroke, the hands push out from the body as if they are trying to push apart the water in front of them. The swimmer's legs kick back together, as if pushing off of a ledge, and his or her face enters the water when all the limbs are stretched out completely. The head bobs back up for a breath as the knees bend and the arms return to the starting position in front of the swimmer's chest.

A swimmer's arms arch out gracefully in front of him or her, like wings, while performing the butterfly stroke. Upper-body movements are similar to those of the crawl, but the arms move together instead of one at a time. The kick is also similar, except that the legs move much faster and in synch with the arms. The butterfly is considered the hardest stroke to master.

Pool Etiquette

When the pool is crowded, swimmers should follow a few polite principles:

- Swim in a lane with people who are at the same speed/ability level.
- Swim counterclockwise in a circle if there are more than two people in a lane.
- Don't follow the swimmer in front too closely.
- Yield the right of way to faster swimmers, and pass slower swimmers on the left after tapping them on the foot.
- Move out of the way when you take a short pause, and out of the pool if you're resting more than a moment.

The sidestroke involves swimmers lying on one side, bending their legs toward their body and then kicking them out at the same time, stretching them straight. The arm that's underwater stretches forward and slices through the water, winding up pressed to the chest. The top arm remains resting above the water, on the swimmer's hip.

Frequency and Timing

Professional swimmers are exciting to watch. They jump off the blocks into large pools, racing against each other and the clock. Those who swim for fun and fitness, however, shouldn't be obsessed with speed. To get health benefits, people need to swim long enough to raise their heart rate for a sustained, or reasonably lengthy, time. Swimming fast will quickly get the heart racing but only for a short burst, so that won't get the job done.

Fitness swimmers want to build endurance instead. Amateur swimmers should gradually increase the amount of time spent working out in the pool before thinking

Proper form trumps speed when people are first learning to swim.

about increasing speed. When it comes to swimming, slow and steady wins the fitness race. Yet that doesn't mean you should never swim fast. Interval training, where swimmers alternate a relaxing pace with short bursts of speed, is a common practice for professional swimmers that can work for amateurs as well. Switching from one stroke to another, either from one session to the next or within a session, will help keep swimming interesting as well.

Coaches, trainers, and doctors recommend people start out slowly when they first begin a fitness routine. Those just getting started in a swimming routine should shoot for ten to twenty minutes of continuous swimming, and no more than thirty minutes in the water at any one time. Three times a week is the recommended routine for swimmers. You can do other exercises and activities on your days off, if you feel like it.

Getting into Gear

The only gear necessary for swimming is a bathing suit, and maybe a towel for drying off afterward. There is additional equipment that swimmers might want to consider using, which can make a water workout more enjoyable and productive.

Goggles are like sunglasses for the pool. They help filter out elements that can get in the way of clear vision. Swimming underwater can be safer with goggles. This type of eyewear encourages swimmers to open their eyes, which lets them avoid bumping into the sides of the pool, other swimmers, or any number of obstacles in the water.

Fins, which go on the feet, are more typically used by divers. Swimmers can make good use of them as well. Also known as flippers, fins can add speed and also help strengthen a person's ankles. Hand paddles, which are like fins for the upper body, increase resistance, which slows down but strengthens the body. Another advantage of this type of gear is that it helps the body achieve a straight and strong body position. The hope is that muscles will remember what proper position feels like and imitate that motion, even when the fins and paddles are removed.

Swimmers hold on to kickboards to strengthen their legs and practice kicking techniques. To give their arms a special workout, swimmers can rest their legs on (or attach them to) pull-buoys, which support the body and keep the legs from kicking.

Swimming and Your Health

Swimming is considered a "whole body" workout. In other words, a person's entire body participates in, and benefits from, this particular water-based exercise. And there are plenty of benefits to be had.

Swimming is one of the very few types of exercise that offer both aerobic and strength training with each workout session. Each of the recognized signs of physical fitness—cardiorespiratory (heart, veins, and lungs) health, muscle strength, endurance, flexibility, and, to a certain degree, weight control—is covered by swimming.

Helping the Heart

The heart is the main recipient of swimming's aerobic benefits. Doing laps—which equal one length of a pool, or a similar, set distance in open water like a lake or a pond—makes the heart pump faster than if a person was simply floating in the water. Beating faster means more blood is being delivered throughout the body and more oxygen is getting to the muscles and organs. Beyond an increase in the total number of beats per minute, swimming also lets the heart circulate more blood with each beat. Some estimates state that swimming allows 10 to 20 percent more blood to flow every time the heart beats.

Although more blood is coursing through a swimmer's

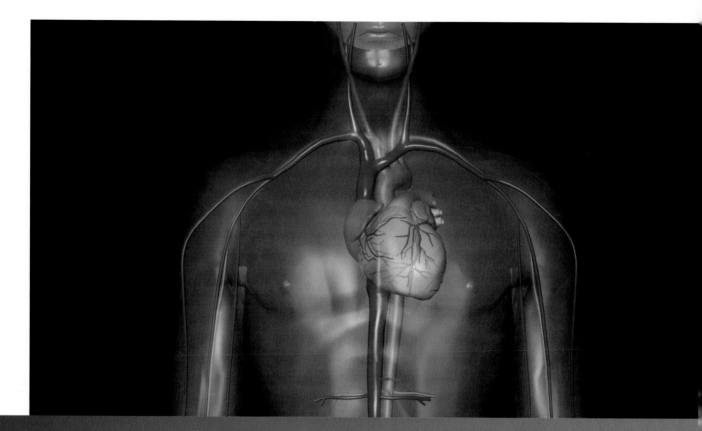

The heart works harder, but feels less pressure, when a person swims regularly.

veins, his or her blood pressure actually drops. Blood pressure measures the force with which blood pushes against the walls of arteries, which are the vessels that transport blood away from the heart. If the pressure is too high, the force of blood flow can damage the arteries. It's as if gallons of water were being forced through a small, thin tube. The tube can't contain such a large amount of rushing water all at once and eventually splits apart because of the pressure. Over time, the damage done by continuous high blood pressure can lead to heart disease, organ failure, and even death.

So the goal of aerobic exercise, such as swimming, is to increase the volume, or amount, of blood that flows but not have it harshly force its way through the arteries.

Breathing Trouble, Swimming Success

U.S. swimmer Amy Van Dyken began swimming because severe asthma kept her from participating in most other childhood games. Today, she is the proud owner of six Olympic gold medals. Despite asthma symptoms, Mark Spitz brought home seven gold medals in 1972. Canadian Brent Hayden wasn't diagnosed as an asthmatic until he was an adult. He managed to swim through coughing fits to become a national and world champion.

As mentioned in chapter 1, a person's blood vessels, which include the arteries, become more flexible and numerous thanks to swimming. Flexible arteries can expand to accommodate greater volumes of blood, so the force is lessened. Additional vessels also take some of the pressure off because there are more pathways for the blood to travel. In other words, there isn't a vessel "traffic jam" because blood has the option of taking various side streets.

Subsequently, a swimmer's blood pressure drops. Keeping blood pressure low is a fitness goal. This helps deliver more vital oxygen throughout the body and also prevents all sorts of heart-related disease.

Breathe More Freely

Aerobic exercise in general helps people get healthier and increases the amount of oxygen absorbed by the body. However, a number of studies have come to the conclusion that swimming is the best exercise for people who have asthma. Symptoms of asthma include swollen bronchioles, which are the airways that allow air to pass into and out of the lungs, and difficulty breathing.

Swimming enlarges the lungs and relaxes the branch-like bronchi. As a result, each timed breath a swimmer takes is more effective at delivering oxygen.

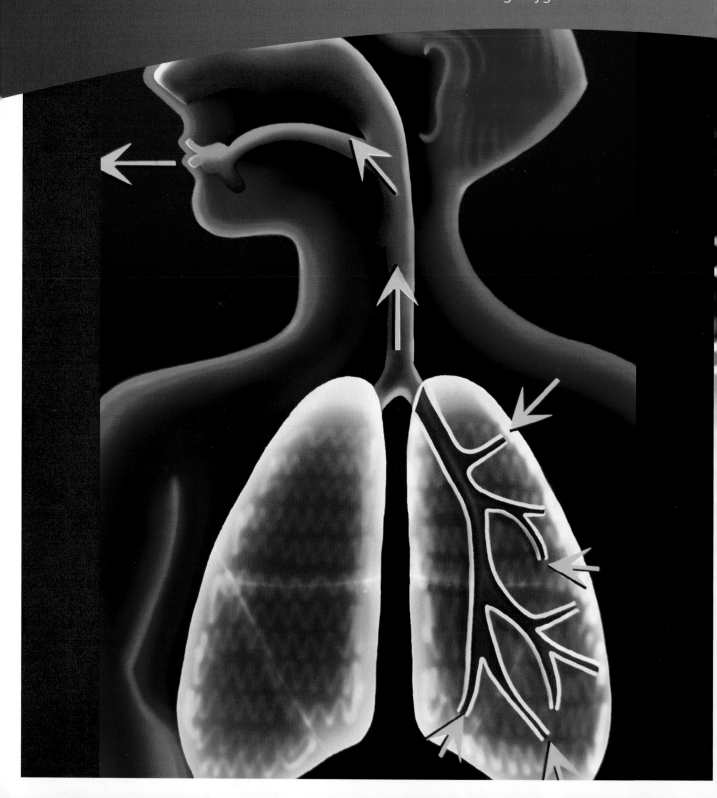

Why swimming helps asthmatics breathe easier remains a mystery, although scientists and medical professionals have some theories. One common belief is that humidity, or moisture, in the air from water in the pool is more soothing to the bronchial tubes than drier air over land. Others claim that the regulated breathing required by swimming somehow balances the amounts of oxygen and carbon dioxide, creating a kind of chemical reaction that relaxes and opens the airways.

Regardless of the reason, lung function definitely improves with regular swimming sessions—for everyone, not just asthmatics. In response to swimming and regulated breathing, the lungs get larger over time and are able to take in more air with ease. They also become much more efficient at their job, which is filtering out carbon dioxide from the air and absorbing much-needed oxygen.

Muscles and Bones

Another way that swimming makes the lungs' job easier is by strengthening respiratory muscles, found in the neck and chest, that help control breathing. In fact, as discussed in chapter 1, swimming is a serious workout for all the major muscle groups in the human body. Muscles get toned, which means firm yet flexible or in the best possible shape. Toned muscles make a person look strong and healthy, but they also serve other fitness purposes. Strong, firm muscles hold bones together better, giving the body great posture.

Another benefit of swimming is that being in water lessens the chance that joints and bones will become injured during exercise. Land exercises, such as running and biking, involve a great deal of impact, which is when bones and joints are strained due to the force of excess weight. Swimming, however, is low impact. Because of its weightlessness effect, buoyancy relieves stress on joints. Less stress on bones means fewer fractures, breaks, or joint damage.

Swimming also builds muscle endurance and flexibility. Endurance refers to the ability to continue performing a task even through stress, and it is a major component of physical fitness. Swimming, or performing some other kind of exercise, for twenty minutes is good, but thirty minutes or an hour is even better. Endurance equals strength and energy, which make even everyday activities easier to handle. Flexibility increases people's range of motion so that they bend and stretch without fear of injury or pain. Also a sign of physical fitness, flexibility creates loose yet strong muscles, which help people feel physically relaxed. An added bonus of endurance and flexibility through water exercise is that they make swimming itself easier and more enjoyable.

Upper-body muscles make swimming possible. Chest and neck muscles assist with breathing, while those in the arms and shoulders are responsible for pull and movement.

Swimming and Weight Loss

As with other aerobic exercise, swimming increases a person's metabolism, which determines calorie burn. The more calories that are burned, the more weight that is lost. However, just how effective swimming is when trying to lose weight has been debated for years.

A study reported in the *American Journal of Sports Medicine* determined that swimming had little to no effect on weight loss. Researchers pitted swimmers against runners and cyclists to see which group lost the most weight. While the other two exercise groups dropped pounds, the swimmers actually gained weight. The leader of the study, professor Grant Gwinup, figured that swimmers gained weight because their appetites had been stimulated by water-cooled temperatures while exercising. (Humans tend to eat more in cooler climates to add body fat, which helps keep them warm.) In other words, swimming made them so hungry that they consumed more calories afterward than they burned off while exercising.

Different studies have shown otherwise. In 1993, the Educational Testing Service in Princeton, New Jersey, found that professional swimmers burned 25 percent more calories than professional runners.

The bottom line is that swimming can help a person lose weight. The trick is that swimmers need to swim at a moderately fast pace, keep at it for at least thirty minutes with very few breaks, and watch what they eat when not exercising.

Avoiding Injury

Because buoyancy greatly reduces the risk of injury to bones and joints, and the fact that it is not a contact sport like football, swimming is considered one of the safest sports around. Still, as with any sport or exercise, there are possible drawbacks to swimming. These can range from minor inconveniences, such as dry skin and bloodshot eyes, to more serious issues like infections, and life-threatening situations, namely drowning.

Chemical Reactions

Normally, people wouldn't think of immersing themselves in chemicals as a healthy thing to do. Yet swimming has definite fitness benefits, even though pools contain chemicals like chlorine. The amount of chlorine in a pool is small enough and diluted, or diminished in strength by being mixed with water, so that it is considered safe. Still, health issues can and do arise because of pool chemicals.

One of the most frequent issues amateur swimmers deal with is eye irritation. Chemicals irritate the eye tissue and cause blood vessels to swell. The result is itchy, red eyes. Many people think that chlorine in swimming pools is to blame for this problem, but the culprit is more likely chemicals called chloramines. These chemicals are produced when organic, or natural, material like dead skin cells and

CHAPTER 4

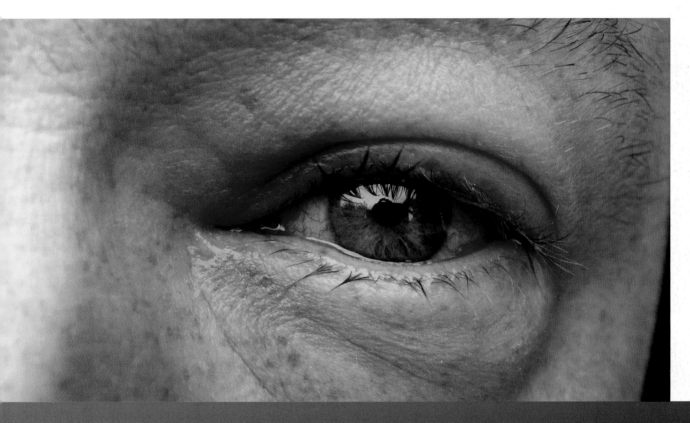

Swimmers can look like they've been crying after a workout. The redness is actually due to chemical irritation.

sweat from swimmers mixes with chlorine. Oddly enough, adding more chlorine to the water can eliminate damaging chloramines. Salt water and bacteria in lakes can also cause eye irritation.

While the act of swimming is good for people with asthma, there is reason to suspect that the chemicals in pools may actually cause breathing problems in young children or bring on asthma attacks in adults. A 2006 study in Belgium showed that children who inhaled indoor swimming pool air for approximately two hours a week developed lung damage equal to that associated with being a heavy smoker. A similar study in Italy proved that exposure to chemicals in swimming pools can

Potential Trouble Spots for Competitive Swimmers

Swimmers who compete professionally or on a school/community team face special health-related issues. Doping is one such issue. The pressure to win can convince competitive swimmers to inject performance-enhancing drugs into their bodies. Steroids and testosterone are often abused by swimmers.

Swimmers are among the most likely competitive athletes to have an eating disorder, such as anorexia or bulimia. They want to keep their bodies thin, which can increase their speed in the water.

make the lungs super-sensitive to allergens and other elements in the air. This type of bronchial hypersensitivity raises a person's risk of developing asthma.

Repetitive Motion Injuries

Joints are cushioned from high-impact stress while swimming, but that doesn't mean they are totally safe from injury. The constant arm movement that keeps a swimmer afloat and moving through water can lead to what is known as a repetitive motion injury. Movements that are repeated over and over again put a strain on muscles and tendons, which are thick ropes of tissue that connect muscle to bone. Eventually, the wear and tear does enough damage to create a repetitive motion injury.

Knee pain from repeated breaststroke kicks are so familiar that doctors sometimes call the injury "breaststroker's knee." But upper-body repetitive motion injuries are more common. Swimmers are most likely to suffer this kind of injury in their shoulder joints. When shoulder tendons become inflamed, meaning swollen, due to overuse, it is called tendonitis. The repeated stress of arm strokes, particularly those that require the arm to reach over the head like the crawl and backstroke, wears

Repeatedly reaching above the head creates shoulder strain, which is one of the most common swimming injuries.

tendons to the point that they can actually tear. Whether simply inflamed or torn, damaged tendons cause a great deal of pain and stiffness.

A similar injury is bursitis. Bursas are sacs of fluid that cushion joints so that bone doesn't rub against bone. Repetitive motion can cause the bursas to swell, getting so large that they can stop joints from being able to move. Pain, tenderness, swelling, and skin warmth are possible signs of bursitis.

Repetitive motion alone is not to blame for such injuries in swimming. Improper technique puts added strain on muscles and joints, causing them to twist and stretch in unnatural ways that are sure to cause injury.

Infections

Chlorine and other chemicals are added to swimming pools in an attempt to keep them clean and free from germs. Bacteria and fungi thrive in water and can enter a

Germs enjoy a day at the beach, too. Open-water sources, such as oceans and lakes, are more likely to contain bacteria and fungi that cause infection.

person's body through water absorbed through the skin, accidentally swallowed or inhaled, and pooled inside the ear canal. Once inside a person, they cause all sorts of infections that can damage tissue, cells, and organs.

Athlete's foot is an infection that frequently affects swimmers. A fungus that lurks in moist places, such as pools and lakes, enters through the bottom of a person's foot. As it eats the dead skin cells on the foot, it causes an infection that makes the skin cracked, red, and itchy. People can help avoid athlete's foot by drying their feet and legs thoroughly after swimming and their post-exercise shower.

Perhaps the most troublesome spot for swimmers, however, is the ear. Infection in this part of the body is so common that it is known as "swimmers' ear." Water that collects in the ear while swimming often stays put, even after a person leaves the pool. Bacteria grow rapidly in this environment. Hearing loss, dizziness, and pain are symptoms of this type of infection. Ear infections can be prevented by draining water from the ear after swimming and drying the head completely.

Drowning

The most lethal potential complication associated with swimming is drowning. In swimming, water can get into the lungs either through the mouth, where it can travel into the windpipe as well as the stomach, or through the nose. Occasionally, all swimmers will accidentally inhale or swallow water and yet not drown. Most of the time, coughing expels, or forces out, small amounts of water from the lungs. Suffocation occurs only when water prevents normal breathing.

Knowing how to swim reduces a person's risk of drowning but doesn't eliminate it completely. For instance, being pulled or trapped underwater, losing consciousness, or plain exhaustion can result in accidental drowning, even if a person is an expert swimmer. There is also a phenomenon known as secondary drowning, which occurs out of the water. Inhaled or swallowed water may not stop breathing right away. Instead, it could remain in the lungs and, over several hours, do enough damage that the lungs stiffen and can no longer absorb and deliver oxygen.

Secondary drowning is more of a threat in salt water, such as that found in the ocean, than freshwater, but it can happen in any body of water. People should not avoid swimming due to fear of this occurrence. Experts say that only 5 percent of drownings are due to secondary drowning. More important, they also stress that even regular drowning does not happen that often nowadays.

Latest Developments in Swimming

The act of swimming has been around practically since time began. It wasn't until the early nineteenth century, though, that it became a competitive sport. The British are credited with first staging formal swimming competitions and formalizing technique and various strokes. Amateurs and everyday citizens took up swimming as a fun pastime in the twentieth century. Public pools and swimming clubs were forming by the thousands across America at this time.

Swimming has grown over the centuries, and it continues to develop today. While the basics of water exercise remain pretty much the same, the gear and competitive techniques have changed and improved. Along the way, both amateur and professional swimmers have racked up some astounding accomplishments.

Gearing Up

Competitive swimmers do a lot of things to make their bodies smoother and sleeker. They try to eliminate drag, which happens when the water resists swimmers and slows down their speed. Some swimmers have even gone so far as to shave their heads and their entire bodies to reduce drag from their hair.

The desire to eliminate drag has created a revolution in swimwear. Today's bathing suits designed for competitive swimming are very streamlined, fitting tightly to

CHAPTER 5

The right swimsuit can give competitive swimmers an edge by decreasing drag and, subsequently, race times.

the skin. Modern stretch fabrics like Lycra are used in suit construction. Some professional swimmers also favor unitards, which are one-piece suits that cover the entire torso like a second skin.

Companies are continually upgrading swimwear. For instance, Speedo has a suit designed with small ridges that imitate the skin of fast-moving sharks. Other recent innovations include suits that wick, or draw off, water and dry quicker, keeping swimmers from being weighed down by water-logged material.

Recently, high-tech swimsuits have been at the center of a major controversy. In 2008, FINA, the international governing body of competitive swimming, launched an investigation into the legality of certain types of swimwear. The organization is

Tools and Toys

Hand paddles, used for training, have undergone redesigns. Today's paddles are molded so that they create even more resistance, making swimmers work even harder to build arm strength. Other new swimming gadgets include devices that count the number of strokes a swimmer takes and calculate the rate at which strokes are taken. There are even waterproof music players that let swimmers listen to tunes while they're exercising.

funding research into whether or not the newest lines of suits create illegal levels of buoyancy, which could give swimmers wearing them an unfair advantage.

Kicking It Up a Notch

Swimmers have a tendency to copy marine life as a way to improve their performance in the water. This makes sense. After all, fish and other such creatures are natural experts when it comes to swimming. In addition to swimsuits made to mimic shark-skin, the world of competitive swimming also has certain techniques patterned after marine life.

Recently, one such maneuver has been making waves at swim meets around the world. The dolphin kick involves keeping the legs and feet together and pumping them up and down from the hips. The move is similar to how a dolphin flicks its back fin to glide through the water. When done properly, the kick lets swimmers stay completely underwater longer on a turn. Underwater swimming helps their speed because breaking through to the surface adds drag and decreases momentum.

The dolphin kick has been around for ages. But because it is a difficult move to master and restrictions have been placed on underwater swimming, the kick has not been used much over the years. Olympic champion Michael Phelps has changed all that, however. When he started winning races and breaking records by using the dolphin kick, other professional swimmers gave the move a try.

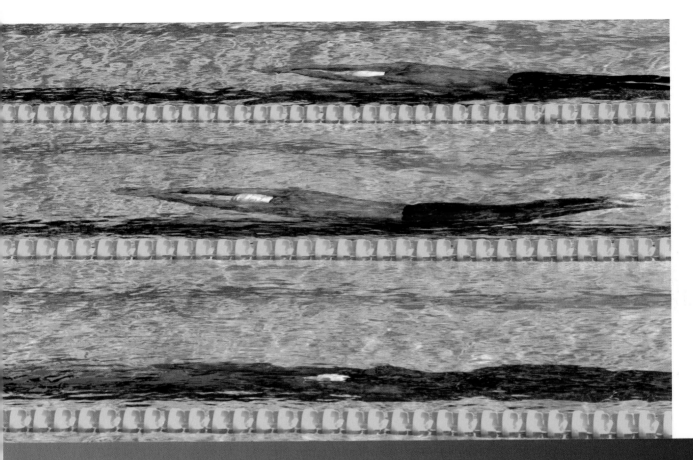

Imitating sea creatures is a trend that is making a comeback. More professional swimmers use the dolphin kick to shave time off their swims.

Meeting New Challenges

Swimmers around the world have been making headlines for taking the sport, and their personal performances in the water, to new levels. In 2007, Slovenian endurance swimmer Martin Strel gained fame as the first man to ever swim the entire length of the Amazon River. Braving piranhas, crocodiles, and the scorching sun, Strel swam the nearly 4,000-mile (6,437 kilometer) river in sixty-seven days. He is also in the *Guinness Book of World Records* for swimming other famous rivers, including the Mississippi, Austria's Danube, and the Yangtze in China.

Multiple medal-winner Michael Phelps has personally been responsible for a huge uptick in swim club memberships and interest in the sport.

In July 2008, Jeffrey Hulett became the latest American swimmer to cross the English Channel, which is between England and France. Swimming across the channel is a difficult and dangerous open-water undertaking, where swimmers face strong tides, cold water temperatures, shipping traffic, and sea menaces like jellyfish. Less than one thousand people have ever completed the journey.

One month later, Michael Phelps made history when he won eight gold medals at the Olympic Games. Often lost in the shuffle is the fact that Phelps also broke seven world records while in Beijing. Experts say that interest in swimming always increases after the Summer Olympics. But after Phelps's performance, the number of people interested in learning to swim or joining a swim club or team has been out of control.

As swimming increases in popularity, as a sport and for fun and fitness, expect to hear even more stories like these in the near future.

GLOSSARY

aerobic Having to do with activity that increases the consumption of oxygen.

arteries Blood vessels that transport blood away from the heart.

bronchioles The passageways that move air into and out of the lungs.

buoyancy The ability to float in water.

bursitis A condition in which sacs of fluid called bursas swell, causing pain and stiffness.

cardio Having to do with the heart.

chloramines Chemicals produced when organic material mixes with chlorine.

contract To get smaller.

density The solidity of an object, based on how closely packed together its atoms are.

epidermis The outermost layer of skin.

hydrated Containing a sufficient amount of water.

immersion The act of being covered with water.

keratin A protein found in skin cells.

metabolism A series of chemical reactions in the body that regulate life-giving processes.

regulated breathing Controlled, rhythmic inhalations and exhalations.

resistance The act of working against something.

respiratory Having to do with the lungs and breathing.

tendonitis A condition in which tendons become inflamed due to overuse or misuse.

unitard One-piece clothing that covers the entire torso like a second skin.

wick To draw off water or another liquid.

FOR MORE INFORMATION

Amateur Swimming Union of the Americas
2 Varbow Place NW
Calgary, AB T3A 0B6
Canada
(403) 288-5693
Web site: http://www.asua-aquatics.org/html/English/indexEn.html
Also known as UANA (Unión Americana de Natación), this organization provides
news, clinics, and a calendar of events for swimming, diving, and other water
sports in North, Central, and South America.

American Red Cross
2025 E Street NW
Washington, DC 20006
(202) 303-5000
Web site: http://www.redcross.org
The American Red Cross provides training and tips on how to be safe in, on, and
around the water. This information is for the national office; for local chapters,
check the phone book.

International Swimming Hall of Fame
One Hall of Fame Drive
Fort Lauderdale, FL 33316
(954) 462-6536
Web site: http://www.ishof.org
The International Swimming Hall of Fame is a not-for-profit educational organization
that promotes the benefits and importance of swimming as a key to fitness,
good health, and quality of life, and the water safety of children.

Sport Information Resource Centre
180 Elgin Street, Suite 1400
Ottawa, ON K2P 2K3
Canada

(800) 665-6413
Web site: http://www.sirc.ca
The Sport Information Resource Centre collects, archives, and shares qualified sport information with sport enthusiasts in Canada and around the world.

U.S. Water Fitness Association
P.O. Box 243279
Boynton Beach, FL 33424-3279
(561) 732-9908
Web site: http://www.uswfa.com
The U.S. Water Fitness Association is a nonprofit, educational organization committed to excellence in aquatics, including water exercise.

Web Sites

Due to the changing nature of Internet links, Rosen Publishing has developed an online list of Web sites related to the subject of this book. This site is updated regularly. Please use this link to access the list:

http://www.rosenlinks.com/hwe/swim

FOR FURTHER READING

Boudreau, Helene. *Swimming Science*. New York, NY: Crabtree Publishing Co., 2009.

Gifford, Clive. *Swimming*. New York, NY: Rosen Publishing Group, 2008.

Laughlin, Terry. *Total Immersion: The Revolutionary Way to Swim Better, Faster, and Easier*. New York, NY: Simon & Schuster, 2004.

Mason, Paul. *How to Improve at Swimming*. New York, NY: Crabtree Publishing Co., 2008.

Montgomery, Jim. *Mastering Swimming* (Masters Athlete). Champaign, IL: Human Kinetics, 2008.

Phelps, Michael. *Beneath the Surface*. Champaign, IL: Sports Publishing LLC, 2008.

Raatma, Lucia. *Water Safety*. Mankato, MN: Child's World, 2003.

Silver, Michael. *Golden Girl: How Natalie Coughlin Fought Back, Challenged Conventional Wisdom, and Became America's Olympic Champion*. Emmaus, PA: Rodale, 2006.

Stager, Joel M. *Swimming*. Indianapolis, IN: Wiley-Blackwell, 2004.

Timblin, Stephen. *Swimming*. Ann Arbor, MI: Cherry Lake Publishing, 2009.

Treays, Rebecca. *Understanding Your Muscles and Bones*. Eveleth, MN: Usborne Books, 2006.

BIBLIOGRAPHY

Arandelovic, M., et al. "Swimming and Persons with Mild Persistent Asthma." *Scientific World Journal*, Vol. 7, August 17, 2007, pp. 1,182–1,188.

Averett, Nancy. "The Crossing." *Masters Athlete*. Retrieved December 17, 2008 (http://www.masters-athlete.com/public/600.cfm?sd=33).

Beard, Lauren. "All About Asthma." *Sport Information Resource Centre Swim News*, December–January 2008, pp. 12–13.

Capri, Anthony, and Martha Marie Day. "Density." *Visionlearning*, Vol. SCI-1 (4). Retrieved December 17, 2008 (http://www.visionlearning.com/library/module_viewer.php?mid=37).

Friel, Joe. *Your First Triathlon*. Boulder, CO: VeloPress, 2006.

Gwinup, Garrett. "Weight Loss Without Dietary Restriction: Efficacy of Different Forms of Aerobic Exercise." *American Journal of Sports Medicine*, Vol. 15, Issue 3, 1987, pp. 275–279.

Juba, Kelvin. *Swimming for Fitness*. Guilford, CT: Globe Pequot Press, 2002.

Kesavachandran, C., H. R. Nair, and S. Shashidhar. "Lung Volumes in Swimmers Performing Different Styles of Swimming." *Indian Journal of Medical Sciences*, Vol. 55, Issue 12, 2001, pp. 669–676.

Kolata, Gina. "The Flutter Over Heart Rate." *New York Times*, Health section, April 10, 2008.

Nieuwenhuijsen, M. J. "The Chlorine Hypothesis: Fact or Fiction?" *Occupational and Environmental Medicine*, Vol. 64, July 2007, pp. 6–7.

President's Council on Physical Fitness and Sports. "Fitness Fundamentals: Guidelines for Personal Exercise Programs." U.S. Department of Health and Human Services. Retrieved December 17, 2008 (http://www.fitness.gov/fitness.htm).

Research Centers, Science Reference Services. "Everyday Mysteries." Library of Congress, March 2007. Retrieved December 17, 2008 (http://www.loc.gov/rr/scitech/mysteries/wrinkles.html).

Russi Sarnataro, Barbara. "Fitness Basics: Swimming Is for Everyone." WebMD, July 2006. Retrieved November 2008 (http://www.webmd.com/fitness-exercise/guide/fitness-basics-swimming-is-for-everyone).

Schauer, Margaret. "How Much Is Too Much? Evaluating the Impact of Swimming Innovations." *USMS Swimmer*, November–December 2006, pp. 26–29.

Shipley, Amy. "A Revolution That Began with a Kick." *Washington Post*, June 20, 2008, p. E1.

Staff reporters. "Get Out of the Pool." *Respiratory Therapy*, Vol. 2, No. 6, December–January 2007/2008, p. 45.

INDEX

About the Author

After suffering back and joint injuries, Jeanne Nagle turned to swimming for exercise. Her interest in the sport has grown and now includes the extensively researched information shared in the pages of this book.

Photo Credits

Cover and interior (silhouetted figures) © www.istockphoto.com/apatrimonio and © www.istockphoto.com/Simon Spoon; cover and interior (stripe graphics) © www. istockphoto.com/Brandon Laufenberg; cover, p. 1 (circulatory system figure) © www.istockphoto.com/Mads Abildgaard; p. 5 John MacDougall/AFP/Getty Images; p. 8 © Mark Miller/Photo Researchers, Inc.; p. 10 © Stephen Frink/Corbis; p. 11 Shutterstock.com; p. 14 © Marc Serota/Corbis; p. 16 © www.istockphoto.com/Gert Vrey; pp. 17, 35 Martin Hunter/Getty Images; p. 19 © www.istockphoto.com/ Dennis Sabo; p. 22 LifeART image © 2010 Lippincott Williams & Wilkins. All rights reserved; p. 24 © Véronique Estiot/Photo Researchers, Inc.; p. 26 © Anatomical Travelogue/Photo Researchers, Inc.; p. 29 Norman Hochheimer/doc-stock/Visuals Unlimited, Inc.; p. 31 Olivier Morin/AFP/Getty Images; p. 32 © James Leynse/Corbis; p. 37 Stan Honda/AFP/Getty Images; p. 38 Shaun Botterill/Getty Images.

Designer: Nicole Russo; Editor: Nicholas Croce;
Photo Researcher: Cindy Reiman

FEB 2010